Metrophobia

an irrational fear of poetry

Carolyn Martin

LINGUA INK BOOKS

Copyright © 2025 by Carolyn Martin
All rights reserved.
Visit the author's website at carolynmartinpoet.com

Author photo by Kathy J. Richard

No part of this publication may be reproduced, distributed, or transmitted in any form or by any means, including photocopying, recording, or other electronic or mechanical methods, without the prior written permission of the publisher, except as permitted by U.S. copyright law. For permission requests, contact info@linguaink.com.

ISBN 979-8-9906749-1-2
LCCN 2025910451

Published by Lingua Ink Books
Portland, Oregon • linguaink.com

Dedication

To Sage Cohen: a wildly talented author/coach/teacher/editor/community alchemist/muse/friend who lives the life poetic elegantly everyday

One of my secret instructions to myself as a poet is: Whatever you do, don't be boring.
—Anne Sexton

Contents

Metrophobia	1
A poem begins with a lump in the throat	2
Dear Writing Coach,	3
To a Librocubicularist	4
Chores	5
From the Chef to the Wannabe	6
What a Poet Desires	7
To: Jay Stormer	8
Ode to Doing Nothing	10
Nothing is improved by being praised	11
Blessing the Feral Cat	12
Right Now	13
Wanted: An Imagined Reader	14
Days Dedicated to Something	16
Maria on the Moon	17
Q&A	19
To My Soon-to-Be-Favorite Advice Columnist	20
Revision	21
Recast	23
Reporting Live	24
Death by Planet	26
Dispatch from Gaza, January 2025	28
Improvisation	29
Penumbra	30
Fishing: Nine Variations on a Theme	31

The Chinwagger's Complaint	32
She's having a crackdown— and other eclectic sayings of an original artist	33
Sight Shifting	34
I have faith in nights	35
You Call It "the Blues"	36
Concurrencies	37
Resilience	38
Sears Automated Response to a Service Call	39
I Love Telling People I Write Poetry	40
Ekphrasis	41
To: Marvin Bell	42
Twenty Working Titles with Epigraphs That May Inspire a Chapbook	43
What the Buddha Said While Reading My Poems	45
Eighty	46

Acknowledgments

About the Author

Reader Thoughts

Metrophobia

—an irrational fear of poetry

This can't be right.
I expected fear
of cities/subways/taxi cabs.
Of bodies pressed to get
somewhere down
noisome streets that reek
of chestnuts/hot dogs/hardhat sweat
and hawkers hawking
faux accessories.
Not of meters and tropes
luring mind-waves to slow,
heart-waves to swell.
Not of "What does it mean?"
posed by teachers
schooled to explicate
fourteen lines
in multi-paragraphs.
Yet, when poems proclaim
humans on this wobbly earth
have muffed their cosmic test
or stir up narratives
of mothers/fathers/uncles/aunts,
the witness they bear
might incite a racing pulse
and wildly startled eyes.

A poem begins with a lump in the throat

—Robert Frost

or with the feral cat befuddled by snow's first fall
   or the song sparrow pouting on a wet-streaked fence
      or the white crab spider beheading a bumble bee

or with Western gulls slapping across the littoral zone
   or foaming waves trying to drown relentless fleas
      or beached seals longing for rogues to guide them home

or with the boyfriend I ditched for habit, veil, and vows
   or my retreat from prayers, promises, and belief
      or abstractions replaying myths of God

or with Buddha's "What's worth doing blossoms from the heart"
   or Muhammad's complement, "Be kind. It beautifies"
      or Nikki Giovanni's claim, "Life is a good idea...."

or with my brother's call from the ICU: "Mom's gone"
   or questions I wanted to ask before she chose to die
      or distressing truth: missing's eclipsed by relief

Dear Writing Coach,

With all due respect to your committed attempts
to focus me on one true project at a time,
I prefer the undisciplined pursuit of more.
When I ease down the road to find a frog
or pick low-hanging figs, I love how my mind
fiddles over dandelions, faded jeans,
and my mother's last phone call.
Not to mention, forget-to-do lists,
a nosey neighbor's sass, or scientific facts
one poem cannot contain. I'm eager
to find homes for sunflowers killed by frost
or bumblebee queens grown weak in early spring.
And those forests moving north each year?
Each deserves the reverence of sonnets
or nonfiction exposés. This is not to say
I'm ungrateful for your blueprinted strategies,
and the way you encourage overcoming fear
is exceptional. But today, I'm re-thinking
the alchemy of promises. This will, I'm sure,
result in a few more incompletes. I'll text you
to schedule a chat about parsing out essentials
in my chapbook, essay, and book review.
I'll count on your focused expertise next week.

—Your Committed Student

To a Librocubicularist

—Someone who reads in bed

Lower your windows and black-out shades.
Porchlights/streetlights/headlights distract,
not to mention the clowder of cats screeching
in heat and kids whining against bedtime.
Grab a bag of popcorn or potato chips
and last week's *New Yorker*, *Time*,
The Sun, and *National Geographic*.
Prop yourself against pillows—three,
maybe four—and alert your pen
to seize pithy words and happenings
you need for poems not yet conceived.
Study Neanderthals' ingenuity
and how "pre-traumatic stress" defines your life.
Follow pink river dolphins down the Amazon
and birds dreaming their songs at night.
Clarify "trans": -vestite, -gender, -sexual,
and challenge the political.
"Earwitness" the snags in AI's creativity
where sonnets mute the human heart
in one-hundred-forty-four syllables.
At 10 p.m., scan your notes.
Pink dolphins delight.
So do Neanderthals weaving rope
by fire glow and the fellow flouncing
women's clothes around his college dorm.
Then at lights out, ask the rising dark
to soothe you into dreams of poems
prancing up the street where birds
practice syllabic streams
navigating through the edges of night.

Chores

This morning you came down the stairs to chide
me for the laundry I forgot to dry
and dabs of Crest I dropped into the sink.
"Memory's slipping," I say, but you think
otherwise: "You're writing poetry!"
Of course! The neighbor's blossomed cherry tree
is fading and bunches of daffodils
are slipping off their elegance near squills
bent in defeat. Although there's more to come—
gardenias, roses, daisies, phlox, and mums—
impermanence had marred another day
and I need to fix each passing-away
in long-lived images. So forgive me,
my dear. You're right. Today's chore? Poetry.

From the Chef to the Wannabe

I'm confused. The master of the microwave
wants to cook? You've called my menus
an abuse of time and hate being told what to do
so this could risk our relationship.
Worth a try? Then let's get on with it.

Who was it who said, "Happiness begins
with an onion?" Respectfully, that's bunk.
It's the sautéed delight of garlic that leads to bliss.
Grab the sharpest knife in the block near the sink
and the red ceramic pan beneath the stove.
Unclove two bulbs and mince them in
the presser to your right.
A woman and her tools, I'm convinced,
are invincible. Now, heat a tablespoon
of extra virgin oil on medium and add...

Wait! Are you word-gathering again?
Predictable: the way your mind swerves
like when we're out for a drive
and your Honda weaves between the lines
and I have to shout you back. No shouting now.
Your urge to write is gathering steam.

I know your eight-piece chicken deals deserve
a light splash of verse, but my Dijon salmon
with cilantro rice would sizzle in an ode.
Go, grab your pad and pen. "The first lesson
of cooking school...." You supply the words.

What a Poet Desires

Not the Pulitzer, National Book Award,
    the *New York Times Best Seller* list,
        pages in the *New Yorker* and *Poet Lore*.

Not a panel seat with Ava, Billy, and Jericho,
    dazzling rapt audiences with strategies
        perfected in a dozen dazzling poems.

Not a Perrier sans ice that waits when she walks
    into an Oprah interview to chat about wars
        raging over her seventh manuscript.

Notoriety exhausts, she knows herself well enough
    to know, so she imagines applause when taking
        out the trash and picking up the mail.

When writing a poem-a-week satisfies
    and one "yes" out of fifteen "sends" feels as right
        as walks around the neighborhood to witness

entanglements like the holly berried in Cyprus trees,
    rampant squirrels bickering with Steller's jays,
        and a yellow lab snookered by a stray black cat.

So tonight, when the local laureate rouses up
    an adoring crowd, she'll lounge in the back row,
        nodding/smiling/taking a few iambic notes.

To: Jay Stormer
Re: Your Painting, "Unsatisfied Externals"
Date: mm/dd/yyyy

Dear Jay,

After contemplating your intriguing piece,
I'd like to know if "externals" mean
the vaguely visible leaf-bare tree
outside your mullioned windowpanes?
I understand why the philodendron
barely holding on to your vacant tabletop
seems "unsatisfied," just like the off-kilter plug
that has nothing to electrify.
But I'm not sure why this framed room,
sketched in black and white, is propped
against a yellow-green wall flowing
into a yellow-green floor. A room
within a room: a hint at externality?

I need to know, Jay, because I'm drafting
a poem called "Sitting Room Without a Fireplace."
The narrator listens to sleet tip-tapping
through your tree and waits for your weary plant
to crash on your rugless floor.
She gets up to stoke a fire only to recall
you didn't sketch a hearth.
She yearns for a book but can't find the library
nor a scrap of anything to write her musings on.
What's left to do? Meditate on the yellow splats—
agitated worms or distorted human shapes?—
dancing through every green-painted space.

That's it so far, Jay, but I suspect the narrator,
patient poet that she is, will struggle with themes

within themes and revisions of revisions
until she's satisfied with reframing your sparsity.

Note: "Unsatisfied Externals" was used as a prompt for *Rattle's* ekphrastic challenge in December 2022. Here's a link to the painting and one of the winning poems: https://rattle.com/the-room-as-we-see-it-by-andrew-payton/

Ode to Doing Nothing

It is beautiful to do nothing and rest afterwards.
—Spanish proverb

Here's to my green reclining chair,
the spider hiking up the wall,
and the philodendron's unfurling leaves.
Kudos to discarded deadlines
and more-to-do lists
inspiring Goodwill trips
with hangers of navy-blue business suits
and boxes of black high heels.

Praise to the switch
from "rush-to-achieve"
to "savoring" the stillness
after brusque gusts of grief
roar by and glaciers of doubt
bury themselves in warming seas.
Not to mention, the relief
of witnessing the world unravel
and re-ravel in the luxury
of blue jeans and polar fleece.

It goes with saying,
blessèd be the unsubtle voice
reminding me
there's always more nothing-to-do
in a restful afterwards—
except, perhaps, to whisper,
"Slow down!"
to herds of impulsive clouds
galloping around the room.

Nothing is improved by being praised

—Carl Dennis, "Canadian Hemlock"

Listen up, Carl. Think again.
My feral cat's green eyes blaze
whenever I praise her cleanliness.
Between naps in bark dust and forays
into bowls of food, she licks and cleans
and preens her mahogany-tinged black coat
growing thick for winter's freeze, reminding me
delicacy in the wild is beyond astonishing.

And consider how my miniature roses blush
when I compliment their autumn rush
from white to yellow-fringed-in-red.
This, after months of watering and urging
new buds to conquer summer heat.
They followed my advice and rose
to heights beyond what experts claim.
Every day we share a bow: mine to their fortitude,
theirs to smiles I can't contain.

Even undeservings, Carl, need an uplift:
slugs brunching on Hosta leaves,
dandelions denying they're weeds,
empty robins' nests clinging to maple trees.
Useful or not, their natural virtue's served
by poets who congratulate them
in a line or two. So give it up, Carl,
for the gnarly hemlock you nearly dismissed.
Think what wildly raucous praise might do!

Blessing the Feral Cat

With thanks to Lucille Clifton

may the cat sleeping in the lavender
shade of a summer afternoon
remind me to lower my voice
below a song sparrow's pitch
in respect for her nocturnalness
and may her grooming rituals
inspire cleaning-out, lightening loads,
freeing me from everything too-much
and may her green eyes
prancing across the yard
as morning opens the sliding door
and breakfast waits on the patio
proclaim she's safe from galivanting
the night around her universe
and may this one relieved poem
be enough to bless any day

Right Now

You might as well decide to start enjoying your life right now, because it's not ever going to get better than right now—until it gets better right now!
—Esther Hicks

By the time the red sky seeps through Douglas firs,
I've tallied up a half-dozen "nows":
t-shirt and jeans tugged on, hair combed,
coffee poured, Special K sogging in a bowl,
news scanned for headlines/deadlines/hopelines,
and the decision to decide
that every slip and slide, cheer and sigh,
needs attention paid so enjoyment can dole
itself out as the day unrolls. Although…
how do we know when a new "now" appears?
A clock's tick? A stiff back seeking a stretch?
A racing thought upending a pondering?

What if earth's Timeline—
from creation myths to discoveries,
catastrophes, and relentless treks
across milestones—were to take a break?
What if it stopped its stride
so we could contemplate why a raindrop
forgets to fall and a ripple on a summer pond
searches for its stone of origin?
What if we decided to enjoy
a song sparrow dueting with a squirrel
or one yellow sweet gum leaf defying winter's bite?
What if we conceived that every better "now"
hides out anywhere in a second's glance?

Wanted: An Imagined Reader

According to *The Poetry Home Repair Manual*,
Ted Kooser says I need you.
I'm embarrassed to admit my computer screen
has been my only audience.
It's clapped for my deletes and cut-and-pastes,
cheered my specificity, bowed to my reliance
on Read Aloud, Thesaurus, and Editor.
When laziness overwhelmed, it didn't object.

So, according to Kooser's Chapter 2,
forget about age/gender/geography
or whether you're a plumber, professor,
or purveyor of intrigue. Rather,
can you sit through tinkerings
of unruly rhymes and iambic monotony?
Can you hike free verse up mountainsides
and wade through unstoppable streams
with sonnets and villanelles?
Can you engage with confessionals
that twist and turn and lead to
"The day I became an orphan was a relief"?

If this job fascinates, please send a photograph
that captures the you of you.
No need to comb your hair or make up your face.
What to wear? Comfy, of course. I was born for jeans.
I'll prop you on the kitchen table against the wine-red vase
blooming artificial pinks and whites.
Before I rev up the day, I'll ask about your night:
did you sleep through the barking dogs?
What about disturbing dreams?
Any plans for today?
(Ted says we're meant to relate.)

One other thing: I may only need you
for a poem or two or, if our energies sync,
a chapbook manuscript. Don't be offended
if, after conversing for a week,
I replace you with another candidate.
(Ted warns about the possibility.)

Days Dedicated to Something

—Oliver Whang, "The Dog (et al.) Days,"
National Geographic, August 2021

Dear Mr. Whang,

I get it: some holidays are designed to save
vultures and rats from infamy; others to applaud
olives, escargot, jellyfish, pigmy hippos,
the Heimlich Maneuver, and hazelnut cake.

You inspired me to track "Fat Bear Week"
and what's the happenchance "Sea-Monkey Day"
falls on May 16? I'll raise my birthday glass
to those briny shrimp and toast their resiliency.

What if I lobbied Congress to calendarize
"Poets Rejected 100 Times a Year,"
"Women of a Certain Age Who Still Dye Their Hair,"
and "Lovers of Hulu and Netflix"?

And might the UN care to raise consciousness
about "Live Sand Dollars on Oregon's Shores"
and "The Extinction of Rational Humanoids"?
Let me know if this sounds feasible.

By the way, my calendar notes today
celebrates "Women's Equality."
I suspect you'd agree one day a year
is never enough for anything.

Maria on the Moon

In 1645, Dutch astronomer Michael van Langren published the first-known map of the Moon referring to the dark spots as "maria"—the Latin word for "seas"—and putting into writing the widely-held view that the marks were oceans on the lunar surface.
—Allison Gasparini with Molly Wasser, *Inside & Out, NASA Science Earth's Moon*

Dear Earthbound Residents,

Although the Colorado has dried up
and every dam in the USA is obsolete,
there's good news for all of you searching
to indulge yourself in water-revived landscapes.
The interstellar branch of the Marriott
is pleased to announce new Moonbow Resorts
on the lunar poles, north and south.

Although our closest neighbor is 100 times
drier than any sandland on Earth,
it boasts seventy-one trillion gallons of H_2O
harvested— easily, scientists say— from sunbelts
and crater-shade. That's enough to fill
our twenty indoor pools for a thousand years
and tamp down the dust on every rockscape.

Reservations are open for Spring 2035.
Call our office in Las Vegas—which,
by the way, now sits on seafront property—
to book your all-inclusive stay.
Prices start at $40-million-a-month
and include transportation to and from,
day trips to Apollo landing sites, and classes
on selenography with emphasis
on the mysteries deep within the core

(...)

and what really exists on the furtive far side.
Permanent residences are also available
for those who want to leave chaotic Earth behind.
Inquire now. Don't delay. They're going faster
than the proverbial cat can fiddle
and a well-bred, athletic cow can jump.

Q&A

The street is still ice upon ice upon ice,
but sleet has finally given up testing
our resolve to let winter be.
We stay away from cars and, if we must,
walk warily to the mailbox and back.
It's garbage night and my green can slides
to the curb when "What are you doing?"
slices through the dusky air.
Our neighbors' six-year-old, wrapped
in a pink bubble coat and glitzy pink boots,
navigates an almost-run across the frozen grass,
and crashes in my arms. "What are you doing?"
asks a toothless grin, framing bright pink gums.
Her first teeth gone the way firsts must go.
Trying to stay upright, I resist a snide,
"What does it look like?" and gentle my words:
"Tomorrow trucks come to pick the garbage up."
Before I can land the period, she volleys back
"Why?" And so begins the daily ritual between
this little Ethiopian and a poet weary of searching
for answers to satisfy. I suspect she gets a kick
watching me struggle for words or, perhaps,
innocent philosopher that she is, understands
that sturdy questions outlast wobbly answers
in the wisdom of the universe.

To My Soon-to-Be-Favorite Advice Columnist

Dear Annie,
I've already shared my distress with Abby
and Miss Manners, but their replies didn't satisfy.
Hence, I'm offering you a chance. First of all,
I like your photograph. Recent? Airbrushed?
Whatever the case, that slight tilt of head
and bleached-white smile inspire confidence,
not to mention your practical advice
about ditching fake friends, evicting slacker kids,
or committing to couples' counseling. So
what I need from you are down-to-earth strategies
to assuage my guilt for wasting time writing
poems for magazines with high acceptance rates
when I could be out pressing dollar bills
into calloused hands or collecting shoes, socks,
and underwear for blue-tarped camps.
The fact is relentless images chase me around the house
demanding to be shaped into free verse, sonnets,
or villanelles, and expect a dozen tinkerings
before they'll deign to call themselves a poem.
Annie, I admit, there's joyful intrigue in waiting
to see what words decide to say, but moving
them around a computer screen exhausts
and unmotivates me to accomplish other things.
Since you're a writer, too—although giving advice
doesn't seem hard when the theme is usually,
"Stop complaining. Take responsibility."—
I'm attaching my latest manuscript. Let me know
if these poems are worth the time or if I should
volunteer for Meals on Wheels, Habitat, or Amnesty
before I hop into my car to scout for "Need Help" signs.

Revision

—The Hebrew, "Vaiyah chein," literally means, "And it was yes!"

In the beginning
God divined
"And it was good"
didn't quite ace
the mating of formless dark
with startling light.
So God put "And it was yes!"
in some translator's ear.
Without a second's thought,
elated land and seas,
plants and trees echoed, "Yes!"
And choirs of sun/moon/stars,
birds, and fish sang, "Yes!"
And wild animals roared, "Yes!"
And male and female sighed, "Yes!"
And the seventh day whispered, "Yes!"

Then God created Time
to buffer each search and find,
vision and reality,
here and heretofore
so the wildest of the wild
could stand in awe
when forests inhaled by fire revived,
enemies broke bread in tattered tents,
hurricanes wiped excess
off this wobbly earth.
And God nodded, "Yes!"
to Before, Now, To-Come
and dubbed them History.
And God created Space
for imaginings:

(...)

wheels and fire, blank cave walls,
sounds that mean, fields that feed,
leaps toward stars,
journeys down arteries.
Then God danced a wild "Yes!"
around every genesis, whirling
them with raucousness
called Creativity.

"Is yes better than good?"
Chaos shouted from somewhere
deepdown the Void.
And, lounging on
the ledge of rest,
God glanced around
at fruit trees, lions, lambs
and the woman's perfect breasts,
and grinned ecstatically,
"Yes! Yes! Oh, Yes!"

Recast

Mary, called Magdalene, from whom seven devils had been cast out. (Luke 8:2)

I knew he wouldn't leave a hole.
Hollowness, he said, is more unbearable
than voices shouting ugly things.
How to say this right? I felt his hand
on my head, then under my chin.
Soft and sweet he was, like on those days
we walked the shore saying words
no one else could hear—not the men
belonging to him, despising me.

The shift? Like a cave suddenly firelit
or a womb touched by unexpected joy
or reflections of my smile in faces of passers-by.
The fact is I was changed when grace—
his mother taught me the word— rushed in
and chased out every shaming thought.
There's more to say after this overwhelm
subsides. Someday I'll write the truth
beneath the facts. Someone may believe.

Reporting Live

Good afternoon, Pete. I'm here at Mount Eremos
where it's been a momentous day. Jesus is strolling
downhill and the wind is kicking up bits
of bread and fish. The smell is...Oh, wait, Pete!
The man of the hour is headed our way.

Do you have a moment, Sir? Our listeners
at home are eager to know how you feel about...
Yes, sitting-room only. Multitudes.
They came from everywhere...A final count?
We'll get those numbers to you as soon as...
Yes! I caught the rhythm of all those "Blesséd be's"!...
"Beatitudes?" Is that a new word?...How about
your stance on anger, lust, divorce, adultery?...
Of course I understand. It's been a long day.
Thanks for stopping by and...

Pete, I have to say: He went on and on up there.
No wonder stomachs growled.
My parents knew his mom and dad back
in the day. Unassuming, quiet, and...
Hold on, Pete! Here come a few stragglers.

Ma'am, could I bother you for a comment
about what you heard?...I know! He's a master
of metaphors like "lilies of the field" and "salt of the earth."
Oh, you're not a fan of poetry?...
I agree. He has a nice smile and the sun did light
up his auburn hair...And yes! His light blue robe
with the white wrap-around contrasted nicely
with the gray rock he sat upon. Folks at home
are sure to appreciate your fashion commentary.
You, Sir. Anything to say about the speech?...

Right! He's shaken up those Pharisees!
Sounds like you'd love to rouse the Temple rabble, too!...
Really? You think He meant "pluck out your eye"
literally or if you call someone a "fool,"
you'll go to hell? I'll have to fact-check His intent.
Excuse me. I want to grab that man
wondering in circles on that rocky path.

Pardon me, Sir...Any thoughts?...A disciple?
You must be very proud...Ah, you're confused...
No pre-speech release?...You're right.
He did sound off-script...He's debriefing
in an upper room? When and where?...

Well, Pete, that's a wrap for what is sure
to go down as "Sermon on the Mount Day."
A few birds are still singing in the olive trees
and the sun is gleaming off the Sea of Galilee.
I'm heading out to find the Master's confab.
I'll press Him to clarify what He meant
about hypocrites, sheep's clothing, and narrow gates.
Tune in for more on this historical event.
I'll be back again live at eight.

Death by Planet

In London in 1632, mortality statistics listed thirteen persons who had succumbed to "planet," more than had been "murdered," or died of "grief." —Natural History, April 2003

Dear Statistics Guy,

For weeks I watched you walk through
foggy London town, pen and parchment jotting
down the why and wherefore I took up residence.
Your one-page report was dead-right.
This year I shuffled 9535 mortal coils off.
You caught my major thieves—
Consumption/Fever/Infant Deaths—
as well as the rarities: one Vomiting,
two Lethargies, seven Murdered, eleven Grief,
and thirteen Planet, a nod to astrology.
When those grieving left-behinds swore
their relatives now constellate nightbound skies
and pray to be wished-upon, you kept your head.
I loved how you resorted to the Bard:
"The fault...is not in our stars"—though underlings
clung tight to their star-crossed maladies.
I almost tousled your tired hair when you growled,
"Lord, what fools these mortals be!"
but settled for following you home.
How comforting: a few brief candles lit,
a hot cup of tea before you hunkered down
to alphabetize "63 Diseases and Casualties."
I couldn't tell you then, and dare to tell you now:
in four hundred years, history will attest
humans killed the planet and were killed by it.
The fact is, the stage is set, the players dressed
to strut their yesterdays across dying stars,
signifying nothing's left of almost everything.

Be what may, that's neither here nor there.
Rest assured that God—or whatever you call
the Infinite—appreciates a job well done
and anticipates another lively report next year.

—TGM

Dispatch from Gaza, January 2025

With thanks to Yasser Abu Rida

The father writes he's home again
with wife and three kids.
"Ceilings, walls, and floors still here.
Our souls were kept safe.
The garden is green,
a color we lost for years."

His two-year-old is confused.
She falls on stone pathways
and, rising up, can't find
sand to brush away.
His sons lie in bed at night
where ceilings block the stars
in a cloud-curated sky.
He asks them if they're afraid.
They dig deep down for bravery.
"Our tent? When will we return?"

After a lifetime away, the father writes
in a language not his own,
in a language foreign hearts
can hardly bear.
"When will my children of war learn
to live inside a house again?"

Update, March 2025
The father writes, "My sons got their wish.
The cease fire ceased. The tent is home again."

Improvisation

The Christmas cactus is confused again.
Its first October bloom defies
a calendar. Perhaps it's found a tune
within a world that's out of sync.

    *

Snow has forgotten when to melt.
Butterflies arrive too late for golden lilies' bloom.
Muskrats wake up earlier and eat
their way into breeding time.

    *

In the year of cicadas, even feral cats
and garter snakes are unnerved
by a trillion unfurling wings
jackhammering the air @100 decibels.

    *

Let us revise answers that need
questioning: the catechism's creed,
the narrowest rules, the narratives sanctified
in science and history books.

    *

What if every person we meet
in a moment of happenchance arrived
like an autumn that can't untell itself?
Perhaps we'd sink into surprise like a kiss.

Penumbra

Per your request, I turned the dish washer on
      and alarmed the doors. I'm heading out annoyed

about the sweet gum tree we cut down last week.
      Gone its shielding shade allowing wicked sun

to scorch marigolds, petunias, zinnias, and phlox.
      Even summer's stingy clouds won't offer sheltering.

I'm off to find an umbrella, tent, or maybe a tarp to tack
      to the fence: anything to circumvent the last

last resort: uproot blooms, risk their death, replant.
      If the solution lies in dirty work, nothing will redeem

our failure to foresee our ineptitude except, perhaps,
      the flicker body-slamming a suet cake or the feral cat—

attentive and pregnant—begging for breakfast at the sliding
      door or the purple smell of irises celebrating

their first bloom: distinctive diversions
      that may take root in the scattered shade of a poem.

Fishing: Nine Variations on a Theme

Consider Wikipedia: "Fishing is the activity of trying to catch fish." Ponder "trying" before you invest in a license, rod, reel, lines, lures, gas, and mileage.

Consider "worm-charming" for live bait. Find a puddle and gently slap your boots to imitate raindrops. Worms will arise curious. Sea gulls invented this strategy.

Consider the Australian scientists who claim that fish sing at dawn. Imagine the reef where they conduct squawks/burbles/pops with background choruses of chirps/trills/caws.

Consider the lesson of salmon: you can go home again. In fact, it's imperative.

Consider the perfect flick of wrist that achieves a perfect arc of line. Land it mid-stream where your "Rainbow Warrior" will court unsuspecting trout.

Consider bioblitzing neighbors' ponds to celebrate savvy koi who outsmart hungry herons every day.

Consider illegal fishing attempts: poisoning, electrocuting, blasting, and ignoring the "Honey Do Lists" your partner angles out each week.

Consider the sturgeon who ran into a concrete wall. "Dam!" she said. So much for this season's caviar.

Consider the word "fishing" first appeared in the 13th century alongside "bait," "boatman," and "folly."

The Chinwagger's Complaint

These fopdoodles don't know diddly-squat.
Their cattywampus minds can't distinguish
dipthongs from dongles, doohickeys from fartleks.
They confuse the mythical with the actual,
mistaking the Washington snallygaster
for snollygosters sitting on their fence.
A two-letter switch defines their ignorance.

On weekends you'll find them at shivoos
where they'll divagate about the demise
of jackalopes and kerfuffle about
gobbledygook. Where one word would do,
they add hundreds more and multiply
syllables. These humblebrags conversate
like klazomaniacs—a spot-on clue
to their snarky brainlessness. A heads-up:
they can't define any word within these lines
so decode as you wish. Purse-proud stampcrabs
will whiffle-whaff about your intelligence.

She's having a crackdown—and other eclectic sayings of an original artist

You made your choice, now make the bed.
That's when the fan will hit the ceiling.

I knew something was wrong, but I couldn't put my foot on it.
I think he chewed off more than he could bite.

That politician seems very fort worth.
He can see the writing on the handle.

Thank you for taking the horn and driving us
to see the "Shimshaw Reduction."

Those are opposite ends of the rectum
and I'm over the hill about it.

Our little dog loves being swallowed
like a sheep in lamb's wool.

My mouth is bigger than my head
and I need another donut like I need a head in my hole.

I won't count my crows before they lay their eggs
and I won't put all my baskets in any one of them.

I don't want to shoot the gun, but there will be
no mammogramed napkins at our wedding!

I just ate two brain muffins so I thought
I could pull the wool over you.

Sight Shifting

A reprobate from Dante's hell sneers
from the tiles on my bathroom floor.
Roman nose, gaunt cheeks, hair blending
into caulk. Unnerved, he wants to know
what right I have to intrude on his suffering.
       *

Standing on our Persian rug, I imagine
deft hands interlacing warps and wefts,
tying knots one by one, row by row.
What's more magical: multi-color geometry
or tribal tales looming in the weave?
       *

How would Monet see my summer yard?
Pink petunias blurring with fuzzy blue stock,
white aster-clusters entwining green,
two gray squirrels darting through a dozen shapes
of shade beneath a smudged maple tree.
       *

While Copernicus claimed a sun-centered galaxy
and Aristarchus argued for planets swirling
methodically, Linus spied Mozart
in a cloud-curated sky and Charlie Brown
memorialized a rubber duckie.
       *

I've written my story so many times
that narratives flow through weary imagery.
Perhaps hints of mystery sift through
multi-worlds hidden beyond my eyes—
each unknown longing for a poem.

I have faith in nights

—Ranier Maria Rilke, "You, Darkness"

when August heat disrupts sleep-fall
and raccoons instruct skunks
about grubs hiding in the lawn

when at-last dreams chauffeur me
to strange airports where shop lights dim
and gates appear and disappear
and I can't recall where I planned to go

when the Blue Moon rises through
Douglas firs struggling to find
unruly stars born a billion years ago

when thirsty words scribbled
at 5 a.m. wake me to praise the last
embrace of dark before the first
trace of dawn stretches and yawns

You Call It "the Blues"

when the couch won't let go—
or maybe it's the computer screen
or nine seasons of *Chicago Med*—
and bags of chips, sea-salted
and stale, grease your fingertips
as the Amazon truck passes by
without the shoes you ordered last week
so you grouse at the disappointing universe
and the neighbors arguing next door
and nestle into a discomfort zone
where you can't coax your bare feet
to slap the floor while Canada geese
honk their way south with a fierce energy
that dismays so you try to remember
what you read yesterday
about how Neanderthals disappeared
and how Earth's rocks can't recall their origins:
a passel of enticing facts that may—
or not—nudge you toward a few
deep sighs and the mild urge to stretch.

Concurrencies

Despite the fact the kids are fighting about who's the next
Wonder Girl and mom's ignored dishes caking in the sink.

Despite the fact she let a week's clothes sulk in the dryer's drum
to track a Steller's jay stealing a squirrel's peanut stash.

Despite each distracting thing, she unearthed a poem and plans
to post it through Submittable to editors with kids of their own

who play with capes and lack fresh underwear: realities
these stressed aesthetes will not reveal when she queries

why her words have sulked for more than half a year
in a poem-shaped hole they call "received."

Resilience

"It's the buoyancy," someone said, "that keeps
you floating on rejection's sea."
I appreciate the thought, but I'd revise it
to "My father's strategy for navigating
waves along the Jersey shore."
When body-surfing tossed/tumbled/crashed
me on the beach—salt stinging scrapes,
sand sagging my bathing suit—he schooled me
how to calculate waves' height and speed
and embrace determined choice: with/over/
under/through. His lessons took.
So when editors toss out "unfortunately's"
or "we didn't have the space" or "we're sure
you'll find another home," dive over/under/
through their words. Then head out to sea
with poems as buoyant as their best.
Float them again and then again

Sears Automated Response to a Service Call

Thank you for calling Sears. Your call is important to us
although, after hearing this message, you may not agree.
Listen carefully since our menu items have changed.
For the dishwasher you bought in 2008, don't press anything.
We've already fixed the pump, heater, and control panel twice.
We're oh-so-done with its servicing. For the clothes washer,
circa 2015, pistons balancing your drum were just replaced
and there's nothing more to do than congratulate you
for slipping in this repair before your warranty expires in a day.
As for your oven, micro, stovetop, and refrig, we have a new plan
for coverage. Only $1500 a year. Press #9 and pull out
your current credit card. We'll process you in record time.

In case you're dismayed by Sears intelligence, my name is Dot,
the affable AI who knows more about you than the FBI.
From your phone number, I can tell where you live and track
where you went to school. I'm flummoxed about the
"Unsatisfactory" in "Conduct" you received in first grade. I hope it
was a wake-up call to mend your rowdy ways. And how did that
Ph.D. in English work out? Didn't seem practical unless you liked
tortured stacks of essay exams and research books. Now I see
you've settled into poetry. Another futile foray into obscurity.
Anyway, if you're curious about other files we've amassed about
your life—as sadly uneventful as it's played out to-date—call
1-800-555-0001. Follow the menu to our astute Customer Care.
You'll undoubtedly be astonished, dumbfounded, and amazed.

I Love Telling People I Write Poetry

just to watch their eyes dart
around the room in search of an escape—
like the couple sipping oak-aged chardonnay
at tonight's gathering.
Before they could retreat, I cornered them
with the only high school poem I tortured out
and Mrs. Driscoll's EXTREMELY MAUDLIN
red-pen-slashed across the page.
At seventeen, I admitted to their frowns,
I didn't know what "maudlin" implied.

Of course—I didn't catch my breath—
my poem was syrupy and soppy,
not to mention saccharine.
What can you expect from an orphan boy
who lost his only coin in snow
stinging along a forlorn street
in a forlorn town in a forlorn long-ago.

Perhaps I was echoing Tiny Tim or Pip,
I explained, as they warily took another sip,
and, like Dickins, I raised my lad to heroics:
Coin found. Boy sees homeless man.
Guess what happens next?

"Poetry lives in the human heart," I assured
my captives before I set them free
and headed for the door, chuckling at their relief.

Ekphrasis

1. Miró's "The Birth of the World" stymies me.
In his genesis, is that a kite or a bird?
Balloons or faceless heads?
A spider stalking a question mark?
Real or surreal? What's the difference?

2. Backgrounded by "The Shepherd Star,"
Breton's peasant girl steadies a potato sack
on her head. Practiced weariness guides her home.
I want to know who will meet her at the door?
Who will brew her tea, butter her bread?

3. In Jesus's painting, the table is round.
Magdalene sits on His right amused by the Matthew/
Mark/Luke fight over narratives. John passes
bread around. "The title?" Judas asks. Jesus gleefully replies,
"The Boss's Dinner." Everyone nods. No surprise.

4. O'Keefe's "New York Street with Moon," 1925.
Ground-level view. Skyscrapers precisely edged.
Cloud-banked moon, haloed street lamp, red traffic light:
a cityscape conceived, she insists, as "felt" not "is."
What is the feel of miles away from desert blooms?

5. Color-pencil on creamy white: "Self-Portrait of a Poet
Aging as She Writes." On her lap, a child laughs.
Beside her desk, a teen practices confidence.
Outside, maple buds whisper the calendar's turn.
They've arrived to vitalize her slowing down.

To: Marvin Bell
Re: Your suggestion: Try to write poems at least one person in the room will hate.
Date: mm/dd/yyyy

Here's the problem as I see it, Mr. Bell:
which poem/person/room? Hate's ubiquitous
and aesthetics make critics of us all.
Take my rift on "Shall I compare thee to a summer's day?"
Cathy complains she's lulled to sleep when iambs
clip-clop across my lines like pilgrims wending
their way to Canterbury's holy site.
Or my homage to a home-bound fly?
Bruce can't conceive how it could read
my mail, much less elude me for six days.
(Wait until he hears about the ant
who critiques my tepid poetry.)
Disbelief's suspension? Not in his glossary.
Wendy says my poems don't turn enough.
Colin says they turn too much.
Pam doesn't understand feral cats.
Patti suggests I study Sexton and Plath.
Meredith urges Ada Limón.
Although Rumi claims he'd sell his tongue
for a thousand ears, I'd settle for plugging
two of mine. With all due respect, Mr. Bell,
a revision is long overdue:
"Write poems at least one person in the room
will love—even if it's only you."

Twenty Working Titles with Epigraphs That May Inspire a Chapbook

What I Failed to Ask My Mother Before She Died
—*The past lies in ashes.*

Forgiveness
—*Let go of hoping for a better past.*

Grief
—*What's love's other name?*

Extravagant Secrecy
—*Leaves camouflage white crab spiders spying on naïve bumblebees.*

Pure Presence
—*The grace of a feral cat stalking annoying squirrels.*

Crabbing on Barnegat Bay with My Polish Aunts
—*Never praise the day until sunset (Polish proverb).*

Recycling
—*A robin's grounded nest: death or flight?*

Subtle Angels Rustle Iris Leaves
—*June cannot be trusted.*

Theatrics
—*Play the Queen though you were born to play the Pawn.*

Karma
—*It is easier to love a thousand people in your mind than one person in your home.*

(...)

"Lost" and "Free"
—*Two sides, same coin?*

If I Were the Creator
—*Stars I held last rites for billions of years ago rise for you tonight.*

It Goes with Saying
—*No matter what I do, I still look the same.*

Perspective
—*I don't care who's right as long as someone is.*

When in Doubt, Punt
—*Lazy is as lazy does.*

Warning
—*Don't get lost in a crowd of virtues.*

What I Fell in Love with Today
—*There's a season for everything.*

Let This Be True
—*Joy is serious business.*

Composition
—*The universe is made of stories not specks of atomic dust.*

Do Not Read This Poem
—*No one has the last word—ever.*

What the Buddha Said While Reading My Poems

When you know yourself, you know everyone.
Shed embarrassment for living a human life
and let your true Self out. Let it out!

Remind yourself that each moment is completely new.
Although you've read a thousand poems,
yours belong only to you.

Learn this from water: the brook splashes loud
but the ocean's depths are calm. Swim deeper
between the lines. Wisdom dives and waits.

A solid rock is unshaken by the wind
and the wise are unshaken by praise or blame.
Be wise: rejections and acceptances are the same.

If you are quiet enough, you will hear the flow
of the universe and feel the meter of discerning winds.
Invite them to blow through your images.

Every poem has a beginning and an ending
somewhere. Make peace with that and wait.
One day the poem will tell you what it wants to say.

When you realize how perfect everything is,
you will tilt your head back and laugh at the sky.
That line deserves a poem! Tilt. Laugh. Write.

There are only two mistakes you can make along
the road: not starting and not going all the way.
You've started. Now go the miles to go.

Eighty

So, I've grown less apparent apparently.
—Marie Howe, "Seventy"

Give it another decade, Marie.
It's my ninth and, apparently,
may be my last shot at expanding
the space around the kid who's hidden out
since the first-grade nun said she talked too much
in class and siblings razzed her about her weight.

I'll discard ancient tendencies:
blushing at any hint I've done something wrong—
like idling too long at a just-turned green—
or squeezing behind friends/rocks/trees
for photos I'd rather forget
or donning my XXL sweat shirts to keep
my apparent abundances in check.

I'll applaud each wrinkle, dark spot,
and white chin hair for showing up:
signs of freedom—apparently—
from roiling years of lust disguised as love,
from rigid beliefs about wrong and right,
from questions about how this life is rolling out.

The truth is I'm getting on with it, Marie—
this letting go of shame for being me.
I've decided to rabble-rouse, razzle-dazzle,
revel in the cacophony of more
and better mistakes during this—
I'm counting on it—best-of-all decades.
I may throw in a dozen humblebrags
and claim my place among the local VIPs
I've apparently been kowtowing to.

As you said Marie, "Poetry
is telling something to someone."
During my next ten telling years,
crowds of someones will applaud the way
I strut shamelessly across any space, shouting
abundant words without an apparent blush.

Acknowledgments

Thanks to the editors of the following journals who believed in these poems enough to publish them, sometimes in a slightly different version with a different title.

And a special thanks to my poetry buddies, Bruce Gunther and Meredith Kirkwood, for making every poem I've written over the past two years so much better.

Amethyst Review: "Eight Things the Buddha Said While Reading My Poetry"

Change Seven: "I have faith in nights"

Confluence: "A poem begins with a lump in the throat" and "Death by Planet"

Dipity: "Blessing the Feral Cat"

Last Stanza Poetry Journal: "Days Dedicated to Something" and "Sight Shifting"

Lit Shark: "Resilience" and "*Nothing is improved by being praised*"

New Verse News: "Dispatch from Gaza"

POETiCA Review: "Ekphrasis"

Prosetrics the Magazine: "Q&A"

Slant: "Improvisation," "Right Now," and "They Call It 'the Blues'"

The Glass Post: "Dear Writing Coach"

The Phare: "Metrophobia"

The Road Not Taken: "Concurrencies"

The San Antonio Review: "The Chinwagger's Complaint"

The Scapegoat Review: "To My Soon To-Be Favorite Advice Columnist"

Third Wednesday: "You Call It 'the Blues'"

Up Your Ars Poetica Anthology: "To: Marvin Bell"

Witcraft: "Sears Automated Response to a Service Call"

About the Author

From New Jersey English teacher to international management trainer; from author of business books to poetry collections; from work addict to devotee of the Spanish proverb, "It is beautiful to do nothing and rest afterwards," Carolyn Martin is blissfully retired—and resting—in Clackamas, Oregon.

A lover of gardening, feral cats, and backyard birds, Martin embraces poetry as her way of interacting with the world—in images, rhythms, sounds, and intensities of language. That is why she's settled into the joyful challenge of translating experience into as few words as possible. Her aesthetic is embodied in Jack Kerouac's comment in *Dharma Bums*: "One day I will find the right words, and they will be simple," and in Galway Kinnell's statement, "To me, poetry is somebody standing up…and saying, with as little concealment as possible, what it is for him or her to be on earth at this moment." Her poems attempt to be simple in language as they grapple with the complexity of being on earth right now.

Since the only poem she wrote in high school was red-pen-slashed "Extremely maudlin," Martin is amazed she has continued to write. Her poems have appeared in more than 200 publications throughout North America, Australia, and Europe, and she has six full-length collections and two chapbooks under her creative belt. She was the winner of the 2025 Hudson-Fowler Prize for Poetry from Central Arkansas University.

Visit Carolyn at carolynmartinpoet.com.

Reader Thoughts

Dear Reader,

If *Metrophobia* made you smile, think, or see poetry in a new way, I'd love to hear from you. Whether it's a quick note or a deeper reflection, knowing how these poems landed with you is a gift every poet desires.

Also, your review will help other readers discover this book and share in the ins-and-outs, ups-and-downs, challenges and triumphs of what it means to be a poet.

Please take a moment to share your thoughts. Even a few words can make a big difference.

**Leave a review at
https://linguaink.com/for-carolyn**

For more poetry updates, visit me at: carolynmartinpoet.com

Thank you for being part of my poetic journey. You are the reason the joy of writing poetry continues to sustain me.

—Carolyn

www.ingramcontent.com/pod-product-compliance
Lightning Source LLC
Chambersburg PA
CBHW071759040426
42446CB00012B/2627